the word *Begat* | beg… *Good* | begat | *God* | begat | *Shod* | begat … | begat | · *Gabrielle* | begat | *Sidney Re*… *ZDA* | begat | *England* | begat | *Glass Lips* … *Dark* |begat| *Mrs Realer* |begat| *Meltdown Wor*… …gat| *The Queue of Dolls* | begat | *God Quid*… …*essiah* | begat | *British Trees* | begat | *Sh*… …*ounty* | begat | *Robin Blood* | begat | … …*ce* | begat | · *Said* |begat| *Allah* |begat| … *Taoists* |begat| *Brian* | begat | *The Son of Glass* | begat | *O*| begat | *Ever* | begat| *Adam* | begat | *The Good Shoes* | begat | *Sullen Suburbs* | begat | *Marion Madder-Layne* | begat| *Shoe-Shine Psalm* | begat | *Good Shoes* |begat| *Mattshoe* | begat | *Shoes of Miles* |begat| *The First & The Last* | begat | *The World* | begat | *The Shodding* |begat | *The Five Thousand* | begat | *Ten Thousand* | begat | *Mandy Realer* | begat | *Little Sids* | begat| *The Messiah of Shoes* | begat | *No* |begat| *Goth* | begat | *Punk* | begat| *Mod* | begat | *Monty* |begat| *The Son* |begat| *That Shods* |begat| *The Son of The Lost & The* our *Unshod* |begat | *MOTHER* | begat | *Nothing* | begat | *Mum* | begat |*Lermin Whiz-Shod* |begat | *Dead Day* |begat| *A Night of Harms* |begat|*Laid Waste* |begat | *The Silence of Spring* | begat |*A Faery's Father* | begat | *The Sun* | begat | *The Moon* | begat | *The Back of Him* | begat | *Round Shoes* | begat | *Swirled Stone* | begat | *My Messiah* | begat | *Out on The Peninsula of Deer* | begat | *Shoes From Your Ears* | begat | *Late Sun* | begat | *Late Rain* | begat | *The Evening's Grey Hound* | begat | *The Dog of Twilight* | begat | *The Again* | begat | *Night's* | begat | *Day* | begat | *My Vision* | begat | · *Land-Fish* | begat | *Earth-Ichthus* | begat | *Heaven* | begat | *Hell* | begat | *A Double-Sexed* · | begat | *The Spit-Shod Mollusc* | begat | *Behold* | begat | *The Whole Snail* | begat | *Wizard of Shod* | begat | *The Hardshod Wise One* | begat | *A Matrix of Grass* | begat | *A White Rabbit Down* | begat | · *Black Hole* | begat | *Alice Oswald* | begat | *Flesh & Bone Things* | begat | *Human Shins* | begat | *The Crossing* | begat | *The Yellow Road* | begat | *Your Son* | begat | *Father* | begat | *Your Father* | begat | *Son* | begat | *The Limping Shrimp* | begat | *The End of The Quest* | begat| *The Wasted Globe* | begat | *The Lame Lad* |begat | *Shoedonia* | begat | *Precinct of Shoes* | begat| *Ourshoerian Legend* | begat | *A Messiah* | begat | *King Our Shoer* | begat | *Mount Shoredon* | begat | *North Face* | begat | *Adam & Eve* | begat | *Various Henges* | begat | *The Golden Cairn* | begat | *The Dapper Tramp* | begat | *Solomon Binding* | begat | *Love of Shod* | begat | *Solomon of Now* | begat | · *Thee* | begat | *The Old Book of The Maybebutmaybenotgone* | begat | *The Song* | begat | *The Song* | begat | *Peter Caughost* | begat | *River Tench* | begat | *The Flowing Stone* | begat | *The Tench* | begat | *The Swoar* | begat | *One Spring Morning* | begat | *Shod's Weight* | begat| *The Shoddess* ·| begat| *Dears* |begat| *Ghost-Lady* |begat| *Night Club* | begat | *Unbuckled Muse* | begat | *William Shapedears* | begat | · *The Syllable Cobbler* | begat | *Five Steps of The Bard* | begat | *Eloise* | begat | *Red Suede Shoe* | begat | *Mad Moaner* | begat |*An Animal Girl* | begat | *Barn* | begat | *The Sinking Moon* | begat | *Olden Stounds* | begat | *Mary* | begat | *Sylvia Laces* | begat | *Ted Shoes* |begat| *The Last of Literary History* |begat| *The Dancing Daffs* | begat | *The Canon* | begat | *The Dead* · | begat | *The Alive* | begat | *Shoe of Union* | begat | *Stayne Badlecloss* | begat | *Sake of The Shod* | begat | *Sold Soles* | begat | *The Easily Led* | begat | *Sproarlin Nasdy* | begat | *Longgone* | begat | *Greek* | begat| *Baader-Meinhof* |begat | *Middle Killer* | begat| *Kid of Victory* | begat |*Losses* |begat | *TSP* |begat| *The Park of Burnt Cars* | begat| *Longgone's Dock-lands* | begat| *Our Lord Sidney Realer* |begat| *The One Who Shods* |begat | *Victory Kidz* | begat | *My Shoe Dude* | begat | *Suede Blues* | begat | *Forgotten Estate* |

begat | AZDA-NASTY · / begat | T-Shirt / begat | Youthful Revolutionary
Revelations /begat| Hard Pressure Press /begat |The Internet /begat| AZ /begat|
NAZI / begat | A to Z / begat | DNA / begat | ADAM / begat | Shod or
Not / begat|The Sermon /begat| Little Middley Boy /begat| Shod has Trodden /beg
at| Spiritual Booty · / begat | The Booty / begat | England's / begat | Lo &
Behold / begat | The First Booty / begat | Under The Viaduct / begat | For Our
Shoes /begat| For Our Lord Shod Sure / begat|Tmpid /begat| The Zone Between /begat |
Now /begat | A Brief Forever / begat| The Figure Forty / begat | · Reflection /
begat| T'Other Shodder / begat | Shoddy /begat | Shifting Forms /begat| The Neon
Lit Livid / begat | The T'Other's Others / begat | The Airbrushed Babe / begat |
Her Glazed Laces / begat | The Final Game Show's Offering of Gifts / begat |
The Utter Camera / begat | Eddy Vaction / begat | SATS / begat | The New Lord
of Prosume / begat | The Last's Temptation / begat | The Postmodern Cobbler /
begat | · Demon Hurtz / begat | The Livid Sole / begat | Hell's Stiletto / begat |
You Shoe-Shagging Shite / begat | The Ground / begat | Stepping Began / begat |
Song of Shoes / begat | The Shoes of Shoes / begat | Solomon's / begat | Scent
Shine / begat | Shoe-Tree / begat | Daughters of Shoeshopingham / begat | The
Pile Beneath the Prophesised Viaduct / begat | The Wardrobe of Solomon / begat |
Rose of Shoe / begat | Lilly of The Laces / begat | · The Shod / begat | The
Polish of My Beloved / begat | The Round Window of Wisdom / begat | The
Lattice / begat | My Loved Shod's / begat | Mountain of Shoedon / begat |
Workshops of Acorns / begat | The Grubs of Oak / begat | Achilles / begat | O
Goddess's /begat| Love / begat| The Road to Dead /begat| The Go-Go Spell /begat|
Sophie / begat | The Dark Shite of The Soul / begat| Holy Shit /begat| First
World Midland City / begat | O Shoeherd / begat | O Husband of Hurt / begat
| Me / begat | Lord of Unworn Footwear / begat | Enoch / begat | Big Black
Book / begat | Enoch The Shearsman / begat | DNA / begat | Jared / begat |
Noah/ begat | Methuselah / begat | · Metatron / begat | Cadair Idris / begat |
Enos / begat | Even The Son of Man / begat | Eros The Lord / begat | Jesus
/ begat | The Whore / begat | Less & Blamed / begat | The Game / begat | The
Woods of Baby / begat | The Lone Blood-Loam / begat | Maybe / begat | O Bless
Her / begat | She / begat | Hawthorn / begat | Sophie Windsor / begat | Sophie &
Sophie's / begat | So Fire am I / begat | Holly Tree / begat | The Great
Mother /begat | Everyone /begat | The Caring Son / begat | The Cunt Mother-
Fucker /begat | Appearance / begat | Song / begat |Everyman / begat | The
World's Oceans of Knowledge / begat | · The Queen / begat | The-Put-Down /
begat | The Put-Upon / begat | · Earth · / begat | The Queen of The Old /
begat | Forgotten Occult / begat | You / begat | Queen / begat | Obscene /
begat | Unseen / begat | Her · / begat | An Other / begat | Her Far
Out / begat | Councillor Sinner /begat | Councillor Barbarous / begat | Shelie-
star / begat | Councillor Coffpot / begat | City Council / begat | The Splitting
/ begat | The Paper Wall / begat | Shitty Council / begat| Cunty Council / begat
| Town & Country /begat| Middley People /begat | County / begat | City /
begat | Golden Idols / begat | Easter Middley Lands / begat | American / begat
|Illegitimate / begat | The Warr-Mart / begat | Shod Vagabonds / begat | Shoe
People / begat | The Tramping Souls / begat | M e t a t r o n ' s Cube /begat|
Methuselah's Granny-Flat /begat |Ol' Nanny Natter / begat | Tom Cobbler / begat |
Troubling Vision /begat | My Shoe Messiah / begat| So Far So Far So Far /begat |
My Lord of Shoes / begat | Shoe Shit / begat | The Stained / begat | Lost Dog
/ begat| Sid's / begat| Dali / begat| Longgone's Bombed-Out Pocket /begat| · The
Old Dark Hole / begat | The House / begat | Presence of Patience / begat |
The Presence / begat| Motionless One /begat | The Three Songs / begat | Lazarus
Hollowshoes /begat | Gone Song One / begat | · Gone Song Two / begat | Holy
Journey / begat | Gone Song Three / begat | The Site of Love /begat | Holy
Loss /begat | The Last /begat |The Supper /begat|Shod-Followers /begat| The Cooked
Shod / begat | New Shoe Apostle / begat | The Bitter Leather / begat | The Oil-

SHOD

Shod

Mark Goodwin

ISBN: 978-0-9565514-1-2

First published July 2010 by:

Nine Arches Press
Great Central Studios
92 Lower Hillmorton Rd
Rugby
Warwickshire
CV21 3TF

www.ninearchespress.com

Printed in Britain by:

MPG Biddles Ltd
24 Rollesby Road
Hardwick Industrial Estate
King's Lynn
Norfolk
PE30 4LS

SHOD

Mark Goodwin

Nine
Arches
Press

Mark Goodwin's third full-length collection is *Shod*. He has previously published two collections with Shearsman Books, *Else* and *Back of A Vast*; and also a chapbook entitled *Distance a Sudden* with Longbarrow Press. He has been fascinated by religions and mysticism since he started writing; being much inspired and informed by the works of Ted Hughes, Peter Redgrove and Penelope Shuttle. Mark lives in Leicestershire, where he works as a community poet.

For Rob

Shoes? It's life and death to me. I had to go all the way to Luton in these.

– Harold Pinter

Mi corazón tendría la forma de un zapato
si cada aldea tuviera una sirena

[...]

No nos salva la gente de las zapaterías, ni los paisajes que se hacen música al encontrar las llaves oxidas.

– Federico Garcia Lorca

Give us five quid. My feet're bleedin' in these shoes.

– from *Sirens*, by Matt Clegg

Let it be known solemnly that the author of this shodspell is not a Christian, a Muslim, a Buddhist, a Jew, nor a Hindu but the author is a none-atheist, a none-believer of none-believing & yet a believer in not believing. Please let it be

known to those

of dogma & quick-temper that humour & its sense is its own form of reverence, for it is said in The Great Book of Clichés: *Mimicry is the sincerest form of flattery.* But let it be known the author of this shodspell means, intends & hopes far more

than the shallows of flattery. The author of this story believes, from his/her crown in the air to his/her feet on the ground, that her/his here given comedy & its tragedy is reverence

for all that rhymes lovingly with **Shod**

The author, being the kind of sinner known as 'poet', can only worship one good/bad, and that bad/good, for better or worse, is

The Word.

the word

is the said & the written & the heard & the read
is read & heard & written & said

word is
the narrow vast

word is
the expanse

yet limit of mind

only touch is un
-touched by

words but words

may ease the strange
pains of touch. If

the word fits, wear it.

Good readings, and may
your God shod you!

Begin at ground

a human does
feet touch

then upwards
towards air

the body goes

•

begin by shoes

this story is
shoe-speech

the speaking
of feet from

their soft
leather shells

feet speaking
good in

the begging

•

each little black circle
between each of this

song's steps

is a hole
through which

to thread
laces like faith

remember

laces can be tugged
tight or not knotted

laces can be threaded
as parallels

like a ladder or crossed
as a sequence of cruxes

•

•

•

First Time

Kneeling
at my feet her hands gently untied
my laces; slipped

my shoe right off

in one neat
expert-shoe-fitter's movement.

My mum nearby but
this stranger was replacing her.

O, then the plastic measuring gadget was cupped
to my socked sensitivity; the little tape tugged
tight lightly tickled

my un-shod in-step in public. Lovely.

•

twenty-seven
years later

the tiny musty
& hard dry

shoe-seed felt
rain in a

man's brain
and grew

from his mouth
rooted through

his feet & future

•

it was Nike herself
she leapt at me
from a shelf

all white & daring
treading air

her robes glowing white
and under those her
glowing underwear

and her wings were huge
white feathery trainers
flapping on her back

I was daft
I asked
where's Gabrielle?

Nike just laughed

the clear gas
of her breath
smacked

Nike laughed at last
laughed

as I did then at every
dazzling white ad
every suddenly colourless
whiter than white
copywriter's line

I laughed

as a dad i did i
laughed as
a dad & a kid

as Nike said:
Sidney Realer If

The Shoe Fits

•

An article in The Guardian started me off.
An article about a homeless bloke. You see,

I noticed in the photo that his shoes, neatly
placed next to his cardboard bed, were exactly

the same as my shoes – shoes I'd bought,
red-hot branded-new, for less then twelve quid

from one of AZDA's nasty massive town-sucking
superstores, clipped on to the city's perimeter

like a fat tick on a once
sleek but now sickly fox.

A homeless guy in my shoes. The next I knew
I was in the small (tight brightly lit) hours, on an aisle,

in a twenty-four hour AZDA, lined
with shelves of cheap shoes. I

had an urge to buy

affordable footwear, a huge urge
to buy vast quantities

of leather uppers & rubber soles. Over
a period of thirty-six weeks of sleepless

nights I bought

shoes in bulk. Thousands of shoes
from sixty-six AZDAs I visited – spread across

just three of England's over
-crowded vacuum-packed counties. To pay

for this, jumping in with both feet, this sudden impulse
to get away with it, this wish to run free, to go

one step beyond – to pay

for this I sold my young burgeoning
advertising agency (Glass Lips Ltd).

And I left my house & its precious contents
of wife & kids. I left them,

my loved ones, alone & only just afloat on a suburban sea.

The first night in a ditch on the rim of the city, the first night
I'd ever not been in a smooth clean bed, I slept through fits

of at first grief, but then, by morning I was warm with glee.
I had unshackled myself from solid illusions, and I knew

that safe in twelve lockups, beneath Stainrail Viaduct,
were piles of sleeping shoes. Now nearly a million of 'em, but

they were as yet ownerless, had never been worn. They
were calm & soft & patient. (They were not

like the piles of worn shoes full
of the ghosts of all those

poor souls lost to the ravenous
middle of the last century.)

So what could I do? I had a secret trove of shoes, and I
was a homeless one. I looked down at my feet's cheap

but neat protective skins. I thought of the skins of the beasts
that my feet now sweated through. I thought of my

homeless other in The Guardian photo. I wondered –
was he at that exact moment wearing the very-very

same shoes as my own? I knew I wouldn't be able to find
him, whoever-he-was-wherever-he-was. But I could find

similar people with similar feet, but feet without similar
shoes to mine. People with cold feet, & itchy feet, & shoes

with soles with holes in them. So, this is what I did:

I decided to begin

a kind pilgrimage
to all the desecrated temples
made of hungry flesh

& aching bones; the temples
of homeless bodies with souls
hunkered deep down

in the bottom of them. Discarded
people with Dark's secrets
kept in the cellars

of selves. Those with holies
of holies, unknown to them
or anyone, enshrouded within

the bile & shit
of their lingering
only-just-living carcases.

I would go

in search,
on foot in hope

of finding
the gleaming ghost

of some hope huddled
in those tabernacles

of the hopeless hidden
behind pungent veils

of hunger & alcohol.

•

So, Mrs Realer, let's go
over it again. You say

you last saw your
husband, Sidney, in the car

park of Meltdown Woebury's
eleventh AZDA, loading

his car with shoes. You shouted
after him as he drove

off, but he didn't, or perhaps

couldn't, or just wouldn't,
notice you. Did your

husband have any cause
to disappear?

Would you say he has
disappeared, or in fact

has actually vanished?
How can you prove

exactly that he ever really
existed? Was he in debt?

Had he behaved
oddly before he left?

Was he agitated?
No. Are you sure,

there's nothing
you can think of that might

have caused him
to behave so strangely?

I see. Don't take this
the wrong way Mrs Realer, but

did you & your
husband have regular sex?

I am sorry Mrs Realer, but it is
my job, I do have to *dare*

to ask that question. Please
calm down. The police

have their reasons
for seeking evidence

of intimacy or
estrangement. Can I see

your I.D. – just a precaution
for your protection. We

have to explore all avenues,
and possibly even certain

orifices. Just gaze into the
retina-scope and we'll confirm

you're you. That's good. Now

Mrs Realer if you don't
mind, if you'd be so kind,

could we bother you for a drop
of your blood. No, no, you don't

understand; that was not
a question – it was a reasonable

legally-binding demand.

•

The Book of Jobs

and for nine months
Sidney did suffer

his Shod's Stamp

his stomach groaned like
leather ripped

as his Shod's tread left
tracks crossing his body

then did Sidney share
with his fellows

whose ghosts were laid
out on the sky's table shim

-mering like layers of ether
whilst their frames were made

            use of

so Sidney did stand
in The Queue of Dolls

as a husk to be filled
by God Quid as

            It

doled out holes for dosh

in return
for souls

and under a brown
winter-dawn fog

Sidney did shuffle

with the un
-done but not

quite yet dead

Sid bobbed
along in the flow

with the wooden-footed

shod in priceless
skins afforded

only through
poisoned mortgages

& the white noise
of digital futures

Sidney witnessed
all the poor transfixed

            by the one

moon of one
coin glued onto

some billion palms

and Sid did know
the sins & miss

-givings & gnashings
& crunching of homes
& the sharp-tugged strings
of puppet-puppeteer

thieves

•

for a second

time Sid was cut
free from real's dream

through Shod
to ground

Sid's limbs hissed
as his feet- & his

wrist-strings burned

his scalp wobbled hot
as an egg on a sun

-seared stone
as he staggered

his soles made the sounds
of stars sucked

into dark holes

a dog barked
and Sid's head

echoed
echoed

as a crow blowing
up on a busy bus

echoed

as a sepulchre opened echoed

as thunder swaying through
smoke from some far

-flung volcano echoed

echoed as a street with homes

gone

•

Sidney Realer the New
Shoe Messiah rests

in a grove of oaks
(the last remnants

of a vast expanse of in
-diginous British Trees

once known as
Shewood's Forest

of Nothingman County)

on a hill that was
long ago dubbed

Robin's Blood.

The lids of Sid's
tired eyes slip

across his vision of
the earth

-ly sol
-id world.

So now & now & now
Sidney Realer the New

Shoe Messiah begins

a dream in which
a female being sings

& shows: Robin pulls
back her fleshy hood

to reveal
her red

glistening tongue,
& the resonating

edges

of her vocal folds. With the bow
of her dreamed throat open

Robin Blood throws
fabulous arrows

of sound. She shows
dreaming Sidney Realer

a dream in a dream;

she shows him
her grim

but mesmerising
furry tale:

Listen

this is the tale
of a lass

called Cindy

who alas had
shoes of glass

glass that shat
-tered as

she strode
and so slashed

her pretty feet
O poor Cindy

Relative

wherever
she went

she left

a trail
of slip

-up red.

Soon found
out she had

a heart

of glass,
& glass

lips that
crazed

as she
kissed

the pussy
boots of

The Purple
Prince of re

-tale & rain.

Robin Blood
winked at

Sid & Said:

The moral
is this:

A Muslim's slippers
are not made of glass

by the grace of Allah
peace be upon him!

And Buddhists' sandals
never have

transparent soles

for the sakes
of philosophies.

And Sun Shon
through glass

does not warm
Taoists' souls.

And the mortal man
named Brian

who lost his
shodding was not

The Son of Glass.

He was just
very naught
-y,

very empty,
very hollow,

all o, all alone

– but he was
followed,

& felt
to be only

for the lowly, and so
hallowed. O

Sidney, love
and shoe who you will!

Sidney Realer only
had this dream one

time but a time
named for Ever

& Adam

•

So, homelessly alone
but strangely not lonely,

and honest as day
relates to night,

to begin my feet's
leathery journey,

I put my best foot forward
followed by my worst

but equally loved.

I put one foot in front of the other
and then the other in front of that

and kept

repeating this simple
repeating this simple
repeating this simple

physical mantra. I trod
on & on. I tramped around

ground – green, brown,
or grey, rural, urban, or rurban.

This just for the just sake
of new secreted footwear
and the great free need to spread

The Good Shoes.

I travelled miles & miles
of open track, path, pavement & road.

Back & forth I went from the stash
of innocent unworn ones

kept safe beneath Stainrail Viaduct. Out
to the streets of the sickly city, back

to the lockups, out
through the rim of Sullen Suburbs, back

to the Viaduct, and out
and out & down into

the straggling fields, scattering

uppers & soles amongst
the soily poor hidden beyond homes.

'New Shoes! New Shoes!' I shouted
into dilapidated shacks, under hedgerows,

and even into big bins
at the back of factories, and crates

of discarded packaging & waste
gathering in the shadows cast

by vast AZDAs.

Soon there were a few & then more
un-homed ones with new shoes, shouting

through woodland & alley alike:
'Yay, The Messiah is here and shoes are us!'

And they all praised and followed me
polishing me with words of gratitude.
And I did shine like the smile
the sun makes to itself

in the sheen of the sea.
And I did beam like the white moon

comfortable as a clean glowing toe
on the road of the night sky.

O on every new shoe a new

homeless face shone reflected
in glistening leather.

And lo! the shod were glad.

•

Out in the fields in a broken barn
I found a vagabond woman.

She sat astride a manky bag
of phosphate & nitrogen-rich fert.

She was naked from below the waste,
and didn't seem much bothered

by my male gaze. I was amazed.
Between her legs was a leather

tongue, and leather uppers, from
which she was tugging

an old wet red sock. The stink
of kipper & vinegar was a

shock.

But it didn't stop me from offering
her a pair of unworn & unowned

AZDA-branded shoes. And so then
she knelt down at my feet, gently

untied the laces of my right shoe,
with reverence removed

the shoe, and then replaced
my blue sock

with that oily red one

she'd just tugged from her
shoe-shaped cunt.

Later on, on the road towards town
she spoke – gave me her name.

O, I was so glad
to have found

& shod

the devoted lady vagabond
– Marion Madder-Layne.

•

Shoe Shine Psalm

he gave
them all

new shoes
he gained

their homeless
following

[chorus:]

his shoe people were
his as he was

their soles' shod
saviour and so

& so

a new spirited
human filled

each new
shoe and so

the group grew

[chorus:]

his shoe people were
his as he was

their Shod's sole
saviour and so

& so

they bothered
no one

for food

they performed

acts of kindness
they ate like

foxes from bins

& badgers
from logs

in woodlands

[chorus:]

his shoe people were
his as he was

their soles' shod
saviour and so

& so

they became
hardened & faith

-full they did

more good

than harm
they shone

through
the communion

of Good Shoes

[chorus:]

his shoe people were
his as he was

their Shod's sole
saviour and so

& so

The Conversion of Mattshoe

Mattshoe – the shoe merchant
something in his looking

me up & down

his eyes on my Shoes of Miles
then his eyes in mine
and his smiling

a miracle

I said to him
Mattshoe you
have done
maths with shoes
for cash

you have through
the gathering
the dispersal
& the exchange
of shoes for dosh
strolled past

The First & The Last

it is time
your stroll stopped
it is time to tax
your soles
on the stones

of The World

kick off
your polished
crocodiles
and slip
into miles
of hardtrod
glad road

forgive
your posh soles

forgive

your selves
Mattshoe

And he kept smiling
And he smiled with me

for every mile

The Shodding of The Five Thousand

Ten Thousand socks
Ten Thousand shoes

Five Thousand shod

•

The Lament of Mandy Realer

Little Sids
is my son

when I heard
it was he
they claimed
to be
The Messiah
of Shoes

I said NO!
he's my son
my only one

a son
normal
& ordinary
like any
mum's son

admittedly
he could be
a naughty
boy and
at times
a bit odd

in his teens
he was a Goth
then a Punk
then a Mod
and had a python
named Monty

but he's just
my son not
The Son
That Shods

he is my
only one

I fell to my knees
I pleaded
wetting the turn-ups
of his jeans
with my tears

that was out
in the fields
in the barn

that was broken

he wouldn't look at me
refused to see me

refused to believe me
refused to believe in me

this I will
not forget
not forget
even when
I am dead

he said:

you're not my mum
and never was

I am The Son
of The Lost
& The Unshod
I am The One

and you Mother

are NOTHING
The Word

is Mum

as a memento
as a hope
of remembering

I pressed into
his palm
his first
tiny shoe

just the one
of two

I keep
the other

like a secret

•

The Vision of Lermin Whiz-Shod

Ah the world ailed me
it seemed a Dead Day
& a Night of Harms

everyway Laid Waste
some day soon every lake
would be sedgeless
in The Silence of Spring

but I tied my laces tight
and tramped towards light

and so & so

I met a man in the mead
A Faery's Father
his hair was frost
and his eyes were drops
of water bright
in his sockets

he was clad in
semi-transparent green that glowed
when he had The Sun or The Moon
at The Back of Him

and on his feet were two
Round Shoes grown
from Swirled Stone

the rain tinkled gently
on his polythene poncho
as he smiled four times

at me with his
pin-prick-pond eyes

he sighed wildly:

Don't cry My Messiah!

his voice was like
a splash in slow-motion:

I had a dream
Out on The Peninsula of Deer
Listen Messiah make
Shoes From Your Ears

Listen listen listen listen

Let the sounds in the woods gleam
I will drop a nut of wisdom
Into the concentric swirl of your shell

Let the Late Sun unload its licence
Let the Late Rain rain through

A hole in your foot

Let The Evening's Grey Hound speed
Let the Dog of Twilight go

to The Again
beginning the edges
of Night's
dancing with Day

I had a dream
Listen to My Vision

Across the ground
But at close range

A strange
Amphibious
Land-Fish

An Earth-Ictheus

A shoe
With a shell

Equally from Heaven
Equally from Hell

A Double-Sexed
Slick motile lip

A gooey locomotive foot
A self-lubricated pied
A little creature of exudates

The Spit-Shod Mollusc

Behold

The Whole Snail

enraptured & amazed I asked

o Wizard of Shod
where should I go
& what should I ask
& to whom should I ask it?

and The Hardshod Wise One answered:

Well you could try

Passing through
A Matrix of Grass

Following A White Rabbit
Down its Black Hole

Or read any forty-two syllables

From any poems
By Alice Oz-wold

But best I suggest

You die for the lack
Of shoe-shined souls

Die for the sins
To do with the Flesh
& Bone Things
Below Human Shins

Die a double death
Die on The Crossing
Of The Yellow Road

Sacrifice your shoes
& your own soles

And when you find
Your Son that's your Father
Your Father that's your Son

The Limping Shrimp
At The End of The Quest
To be blessed & to bless
The Wasted Globe

You must ask
Of The Lame Lad

For whom
does The Whole Snail

show?

And to whom does

The Whole Snail

swerve?

•

Sidney in Shoedonia

Lermin Whiz-Shod had told
me many fables & myths

about the Precinct of Shoes
& Ourshoerian Legend

so I found myself & a
self of me I'd not found

high up on a cliff

my AZDA-fantastic soles
did not stick best

to the slippery rock

far below me a little llyn blinked
at me every time the mist split

a watery eye amongst the boulders
amazed at the sight of A Messiah

spread-eagled on a crag still
as a man nailed to a tree

I'd gone in search of the vast
stone & snow-capped grave

of King Ourshoer and so

there I was clinging to the hard grey skin
of Mount Shoedon's North Face wishing

for Adam & Eve & Various Henges

O wishing so hard to be sitting
on The Golden Cairn on the summit of Shoedon

and then

a man abseiled down to me
with the agility of an angel

he descended out of the mist
and dangled next to me on elastic

he was The Dapper Tramp
he was Solomon Binding

of whom Lermin had warned

he was clad in ripped & tatty
but one-time top-of-the-range

technical climbers' clothing
only his shoes glowed

I'd never seen anything like them
I almost in an unsaintly

way envied the way

his feet
stuck
to the
rock
and made

a snick
sound
each time
his soles
released

Solomon Binding rescued me
yes! a mortal man saved a saviour

on Shoedon's Summit I was wary
of being tested out of doors

with charisma & gifts against hunger

but all Solomon did was give oaths
and bound himself with love

to the Love of Shod

could I have misheard
Lermin's warning words?

but Solomon said:

If you My Messiah had not been afraid
on The Shoedon North Face

if you'd shown the stone arrogance

and danced a tango for one
I would've been

not this Solomon of Now

If you My Messiah had not been wary
of my legend & presence but instead

had believed in me instantly
I would now not be

The Solomon Binding
Beholden to Thee

We sat together in the mouth of his tent
the mist had lifted & the snow was golden

as the sun sank into another world far away
the gold-stained snow around us glowed

& the late choughs' blue feathers gleamed

they were alive blue flying shoes
with beaks & diamond eyes

wheeling in the sky

as I drank hot tea and ate a block of chocolate
with the cold air on my cheeks

but heat in my body
Solomon sang a song from

The Old Book of The Maybebutmaybenotgone:

Song of Shoes

I am The Shoes of Shoes,
which are Solomon's. Let him polish
me with the oil from his brow, for his gloss
is better than sunshine.

Because of the fragrance of thy ointment buffed
upon me, thy name
is Scent Shine, therefore do the virgin shoes
love thy feet. Stretch me,
with your Shoe-Tree, and I will run
& rejoice with thy feet through
gardens & woods, and across mountains alike.

I am leather, but comely, O ye Daughters
of Shoeshopingham, as The Pile Beneath
the Prophesised Viaduct, and as in the abundant
bottom of The Wardrobe of Solomon.

Look not upon me, because I am leather,
but put me upon thy feet for I
am thy soles.

I am the Rose of Shoe, and the Lilly of The Laces.

As the strong shoes among thorns, so
is my love among The Shod.
As the tongue that tightens to the fruit of the foot, so is
my beloved among The Shod.
His left foot is in my left purse, and his right
foot is my right, tight.
The Polish of My Beloved, behold, cometh
glinting off llyns, he cometh leaping upon
the mountains, with both of me tight on his feet.

Looketh fourth through The Round Window
of Wisdom, through The Lattice see
him shoeing himself with my flesh.

Take us the socked foxes, the little foxes that chew & spoil,
for our shodding is tender.
My Loved Shod's feet are mine and my leather is his.
Until the day break, and the unshod shadows flee, turn
my Loved Shod, and be thou like the shoe young
on the mountain.

Behold, thou art fair, my shoes, behold thou art shoes as fast
as a flock of goats over the Mountain of Shoedon.
Thy laces are like soft strands of moss, which have been spun
& woven in the Workshops of Acorns by The Grubs of Oak.
Thy eyelets are like the sweet slots in which nestle
the seeds of the pomegranate.
Thy tongues are like scarlet leaves fallen from speaking
trees, and thy squeak as I walk in thee is comely.
Thy heel is like the shield that should have been
fashioned for Achilles.
Thy two toe-caps are as sleek & pert as the twin otters
that fish among the lilies.
How beautiful are thee, shoes for feet, O Goddess's daughters,
the joints of thy soft foot-slots smooth as the gleam
of jewels, the work of the hands of a cunning cobbler.

O Solomon set me twin shoes as seals
upon thy feet, for Love is as strong
as The Road to Dead we must follow. O
my Loved Shod! for every one
of thy steps you make

in me is my bliss.

•

Peter Eaughost

By the broad rushing
River Tench is where
I met The Flowing Stone

of a man.

He was wallowing
in the shallows & black
mud at the river's edge.

When I shook his hand
I felt his fingers were webbed.

Wet light he had, like a faery's.
And his feet were number nine.

O my... he was of all
rivers from Dhart to Lihnn
from Clide to Tine.

He made a meal for me
from his river's speeding splinters.
And all the while we ate
he smiled at me and whispered:

My prrrrrecious fishes.

And eloquently as his flowing home
he spoke a mysterious parable.
It was like listening to ripples
spreading over a river's depths.

His story told
of a man who
had two huge
fish for shoes

who married

a woman whose
shoes were sea
-through &
sploshy but never
-theless shod her.

And also he moaned
& ranted sadly
about those who claimed
to own all the rivers'
ever-wet & ever-passing
malleable refrains.

But he laughed
his fishy tales
of how officials failed
to chase away
his slippery shape
from the shores
of his loved river homes

– The Tench & The Swoar.

One Spring Morning
Peter Eaughost spoke
with a voice like
steam rising through reeds,

and with eyes filled
with teaming tiny
gleaming fish.

Peter said:

> There are times
> when an otter is not
> an otter and a river is.
>
> There are times
> when a river is all in,
> and the banks
> & trees & fields
> & villages & roads & cities
> are all out
> & vaguely gone ...
>
> There are times
> *when water's attentiveness*
> *is tight enough*
> to take Shod's Weight.
>
> And times
> when water's prayer
> is pliable enough
>
> to produce shoes
> to shod the sure
> foot
>
> falls of The
>
> Shoddesss.
>
> •

Sidney Hears The Postmodern Ghost-Lady

what songy sound from where?
from some distant grove
or from some hot-heart filled
diamond-studded ace of a Night Club?

the song came on the air

did it come like the Unbuckled Muse
on to the golden tongue
of William Shapedears & his
sweet sole-printed pages?

hark! tis it not
the ink-splattered last
of The Syllable Cobbler that now
clinks & sparks
his marching metre of verses?

are these the felt breathy & leathery
Five Steps of The Bard?

I fear not! yet nevertheless me thinks
the song lingers like footmarks across
dewy grass in the shade of a church
& its shoe trees – is this the sweet

noise of Eloise
bemoaning the fatal
trodden trail
of her love

& tragedy of bent
-over shoe-tacks
& crossed stars?

        uh-huh

        don't you press you
        against my Red Suede Shoe!

no none of those above
are the noise below

what follows like lost footsteps
in a loop of wolfy woods

are the bitter & tangy lyrics
of Mad Moaner the shapely
shape-shifting shoe-fitter singer

this is her or rather not her
latest incarnation

lets give a big
smacking together of feet
for Mad Moaner as An
Animal Girl and
her latest

number one song:

Barn of The Sinking Moon

There is a barn in Olden Stounds
They named the Sinking Moon
It'll be the wrecking of summer's raw girls
So Mary knows I'm done

My daddy is a shearsman
He sews my old red gown
My mummy is a prophet's whore
Down in Olden Stounds

Now the lonely one the prophet reads
Is a dress-shape made of seed
And the lonely space she occupies
Is where she's caged and eats

Ah daddy show your fathers
How to be where I have been
Buy their deaths with coin & mimicry
In The Barn of the Sinking Moon

Well, I've lost one hand on the anvil
The other hand in the grain
I'm coming out of Olden Stounds

To undress
swollen pain

Hell, there is a barn in Olden Stounds
Men dubbed The Sinking Moon

It'll hold the bleeding
of summer's sore girls

For Mary's song is done

•

Sidney Hears The Literary Myth of Sylvia Last & Ted Shoes

I trampled lonely
as a carrier-bag blown
upon a digitally

manipulated wind

and then all at once
I stumbled on a gang
of literary daffs

I listened to
the syllables
of their picnic
from beneath
the thick twisting
& prickly protection
of a hawthorn

they smelled
clean as paper
on the page
of their blanket
delicately picking
at myth-bits
arranged on
paper party-plates

as they dabbed
their lips
with white
printless napkins

this is the myth
they ate:

on The Last of Literary History
it is we The Dancing Daffs
who cobbled The Canon
from the leather of The Dead
as well

as the leather of The Alive

remember once
we stretched a rich rustic hide
across the steel of our appraisal
and we stitched his footsteps
and laced his eyelets
with the thread of a lady

and then when
this Shoe of Union
shone with sound

we ripped the rand
and pulled

the threads & laces out
and left the naked

& painful sole
in a puddle of gold.

•

The Activist Stayne Badleeloss

At the time of The Shoe Messiah
there was another preaching
for the Sake of The Shod

or so it seemed
to the Sold Soles
& The Easily Led

he had a faint beard
and was no more
than a boy

nicknamed Stayne

like Sidney he'd chosen
homelessness & the road
but not the woods
nor the fields

he stayed close to home
he preached the backstreets
of Meltdown Woebury
& Sproarlin Nastly

and on each
new moon
commuted
by train to
Longgone

his feet sported neat
white ever-clean
street-sneakers badged
with a classical
Greek motif

he had a whiff
of Baader-Meinhof
about him a whiff
of Middle Killer
he was a Kid of Victory

he'd secreted a sword
under his long black
tatty leather jacket

a huge crowd of young
and even old Losses gathered
round The Sneaker Preacher

in The Park of Burnt Cars
in a rim-estate to the east
of Longgone's Docklands

Our Lord Sidney Realer listened
to Stayne with a crease
in his brow a crease
that threatened to split
like unfed leather

Badleeloss knowing
he was in the presence
of The One Who Shods

untied the laces of his mouth
and released his tongue:

> Okay Victory Kidz this is
> some of my fresh
>
> I'll give you a trinity
> of verses to do with identity
>
> & theft!

Badleeloss's verses twirled out
from his mouth like wasps from

a badly fallen apple and

what's worse wasps fake as
sweet-wrappers badly fashioned

into twee bling
but with a sick sting

> So My Messiah
> My Shoe Dude
> what do you think
> of my Suede Blues?

Tired & sad Sidney replied:

lad your verses are no good
but could be good for the free

if not ruined
by the unkind

glint in your eye
& that wire

of violence in your throat

there are kids who commit
crimes to survive their unloved minds
like kids who belong to this
Forgotten Estate
this sad estate that doesn't belong
kids who should be forgiven

but you son are not one of them

you should know
better and shoe
good

at that the gathered crowd booo'd.

Badleeloss on a role now yawped:

listen Victory Kidz this is
my latest AZDA-NASTY chant
imagine a fat AZDA manager
speaking his advert
look great on a T-Shirt:

why pay more?
let the poor
& unfree pay
more

for you
so you
are free
to pay less
for me

and what about this Kidz?
a little bit more difficult
a little bit postmodernist
a bit more hard-bitten
I learned some of these
techniques whilst at uni this
is an extract from my forth
-coming book

Youthful Revolutionary Revelations

to be published by Hard Pressure Press
extracts available on The Internet:

at AZDA's beginning is
the beginning & end

the same AZ as in NAZI
from A to Z through DNA

all of us eventually dead
ignore the poor & begging for

beginning ends dead ADAM

At this Sidney stood in rage
and the crowd somehow
whether Shod or Not

had to unlace
the shoeshapes
of their ears

and hear him
and hear him
and hear him

The Sermon on The Forgotten Estate

Listen to me now
Little Middley Boy
listen all you crowds
listen to me carefully

let he or she here
who is without
labels themselves

cast the first shoe

at other
labelled selves

show only forgiveness
for the sins we share
with the masses

repent to our
selves for our
repeating &
repeated selves

and wear on our feet
only shoes with soles

we've striven to fashion
from the cracked & sore

cheeks of our own
repeatedly turned
& hurt faces

forgive all us slaves
whose only choices
are to be

homeless or shop

And yes yes I say
to you even show
AZDA forgiveness

through me
and through
you too

if you do
not forget

Shod has Said
and Shod has Trodden

don't let it ever
be forgotten
from whence
came your saviour's
Spiritual Booty

The Booty that paves
the way for eventual
eternal beauty

o The Booty
that for ever more walks
upon England's brownfield
sites & grey satellite estates

Lo & Behold
though shalt
not be shod
blessed

if you forget

the mysterious irony
of that that begot
The First Booty
Under The Viaduct

Shod has shod us all
in his own shoes
first bought

from AZDA's
superstores.

•

And as Sidney walked
away he made
his prayer:

> For Our Shoes
> Let us not forget
> Our neighbours' soles
>
> For Our Lord Shod Sure
> Let us not forget
> Our neighbours' hearts
> Worn on work's & waste's walk
>
> Let me not forget

Sidney Tempted

Sidney did wander
unshod & alone through
The Zone Between

now & Now

he did enter the agro
-business prairies fused
with the industrial
wastes fused
with the gaudy precincts
of consuming fused

with each of his
barefoot steps through

A Brief Forever

and Sidney did tie
bright white laces
to poets' hazelnuts
and did throw

them through The Zone
Between to find
his way

Sidney in The Zone
Between towards
the end of The Figure
Forty did finally face

his Reflection

in a pool of polish
full of polished shoes

And lo from the pool rose

T'Other Shodder
& T'Other's Shoddy

Shifting Forms

The Neon Lit Livid
and in turns all
The T'Other's Others
and in turn

The Airbrushed Babe

and she did offer him
Her Glazed Laces
and she did host

The Final Game Show's
Offering of Gifts
and in turn

The Utter Camera

made of speaking meat
to record & display
Sidney's fame
to The World's
billions forever
and in turn

Eddy Vacation saying:

Messiah I offer whole
nations of slave children
saturated with facts
tested to near death
with SATs & washed
clean of all instincts
beholden only to you
The New Lord
of Prosume
and in turn

The Last's Temptation –

a human skeleton-foot
encrusted in diamonds
fashioned exquisitely by
The Postmodern Cobbler
Demon Hurtz

but Sidney did shun
The Livid Sole & all
his/its/hers namesakes
& shoemakes

as Hell's Stiletto yelled:
You Shoe-Shagging Shite!

Sidney Realer did turn
on his heel

to run

back to The Ground
where Stepping Began

•

The Go-Go Spell According to Sophie

If you can listen

to this if
you can really
really read it if
you can take
this shit
& make grace
then you may
be able to stand
the pain of all
the saints

trudging
the world's
digestive tract
passing
their selves
through

The Dark Shite
of The Soul.

But be
warned

I

The Messiah
of Shoes cannot
listen to this
that I saw & felt
& now tell (&

that goes too
for some un
-known poet
now writing
& who wrote

& who
reads &
who read
this tragic
& nasty

alliterating
Holy Shit.)

In a dank
& unlit alley
in a First World
Midland City

I found a nearly
dead & bleeding
sixteen year-old
underworld girl

most of her bones
were broken She
was cruelly bruised
from her once

-pretty head
to her bare
cigarette
-burned feet

the scraps of rags
clinging to her
that passed
for clothes and
were painfully
revealing stank

of piss
& shit

and were stained
with semen.

I fell to my knees
cracking each
brittle patella
and I wept

wet laces down
my shoe-shaped cheeks

but she she she

she lifted her head
and shone on
and her kind smile
glowed through the alley

she said to me:

O Shoeherd
O Husband of Hurt

up off your knees
let them be healed

do not weep for me
be glad for the bad

& the ugly & sad
millions of helpless

men who each
in their own
cruel or kind
ways have known

Me

Yes my Lord
of Unworn
Footwear
I am indeed
only just
sixteen legally
allowed now
to vow
& make

my selves
open to men

you know
what they say –

old enough to bleed

old enough to read Enoch
and o indeed & in deeds

bad or good or old
as the hills I'm old

enough to need

long long ago I was clapped
between the clappers of

the Big Black Book

it was Enoch The Shearsman
who thrust with his needle
and ran a thread
of his semen through me
mixed the red of my thread
with his grey DNA

mixed Me with names

like Jared & Noah
Methuselah & Metatron
Cadair Idris & Solomon
Adam & Enos & Even
The Son of Man

& not to mention
of course
Eros The Lord

sixteen &
I've been seen
to by millions
& been seen
nude & alone

I know I know

the hole
between

my legs
is so sore
& on fire
it's seen miles
of tramping
it's like
a blackened
ballet slipper
split & lost
& left on
the hardcore
beyond
the hardshoulder

You see me
please for Jesus
don't weep
you see
you instantly
know my names
& yet you know

I'm nameless

I am The Whore
that is Less & Blamed
I am The Game
in The Woods of Baby
I am The Lone
Blood-Loam of Maybe

O Bless Her! She then reached
out her broken fingers
to me in a gesture

.....

... a gesture of ...
I'm not sure what

She spoke again
with a voice like
a plastic carrier-bag
filtering wind
caught in a Hawthorn:

I am Sophie Windsor

here my name
in the wind sir
my sore hole sir
just here sir
between here &
there & between this
thigh & that sir
it's a hot hole sir
a hole all sirs
wish to win sir
a wise sore hole sir
so fiery are the miles
the male miles
that have travelled
along this slot
this rut this slit this

canal of carnal gold

so sir I'm on fire
so fiery is

Sophie & Sophie's
old old royal hole

So Fire am I

Then even though
Her bones were broken
She suddenly stood
up and stared me
in the face
a glare of infinite
compassion terrible
& consuming

She declared with
a voice like
lightening striking
a glittering Holly Tree:

I am The Great Mother
of Everyone from
The Caring Son
to The Cunt Mother-Fucker

But for the purpose
of this Appearance
& Song:

I am Everyman's
sweet & inside
deep-down daughter

raped & lost
in The World's

Oceans of Knowledge.

I appear here
as The Queen
of The-Put-Down
& The Put-Upon

& those put upon
this Earth to be
hurtfully fucked

I am The Queen
of The Old
& Forgotten Occult

It is Me
You see She
who has always

been
Queen

of the unseen Obscene
& the obscene Unseen

After She'd finished
her singing

I bid Her walk
with me and She wore

my shoes

and for miles
& miles I

walked at Her side
with bare feet

& tears

and then She reminded me
that we'd already met

that we'd known each other
from early on in The Song

that I'd found Her all
ready or An Other

of Her Far Out

of town in
a broken barn

astride a fert bag
giving birth

to blood.

•

Councillor Sinner & Councillor Barbarous
had just been discussing the cutting of services.

Now they were about to vigorously get stuck
into the fat matter of raising their wages

for so diligently presiding over the vacuum
-packed county of Sheliestar, and its contents

of cramped & mesmerised consuming humans. But
Sinner & Barbarous were suddenly rudely

interrupted by the unannounced highly surprising arrival
of Councillor Coffpot of the City Council. (Never

since The Splitting had councillors from either
side of The Paper Wall even winked at each

other, never mind spoken.)

'What the fuck?!' spluttered Sinner, 'am I high,
is this some kind of bad trip? What's just

entered our boardroom appears to have the form
of Councillor Coffpot from the Shitty Council.'

'It's no fat-cat's sour-cream dream Sinner, it is me
Coffpot, and you fuckers at the Cunty Council

better listen. There's a real-real big problem, in Town
& Country, and the Middley People of our County

& our City need us, for once, to pool our resources
and, God help us, work... yes, work I said, and what's

more work together!'

Barbarous glares as if a wisp of some poverty-stricken kid
had just hissed out from the slippery lips of his wallet

and stung his sweating forehead. 'Golden Idols, & Jesus's
blind eyes!' Barbarous cries, 'what in this land

could warrant our making cross-authority plans?'

Coffpot's voice falters as he utters: 'Some fruitcake
Messiah of Shoes that thinks he can save souls

with soles he saved

from sixty-six AZDAs around the Easter Middley Lands. Have
you not heard of this homeless loon & his growing band?

I've had a manager with an American accent from AZDA
on the blower for the last three hours going on about how

this blasphemous band is bad for business, how certain
rebellious middle-class kids are now as we speak printing

tee-shirts with seditious slogans, the worst of which is:

I'm no nasty AZDA
back-pocket-patting

BASTARD!

The Warr-Mart man demands a plan. If we don't comply
he's threatening to empty

the fat back
pockets of a

thousand councillors

starting with us
three first because

of our top ranks.
The name of The One

we're after is Sidney Realer, one

-time advertising copywriter, & rising businessman
suddenly turned nuts – overnight developed some kind

of religious shoe-fetish. And worst the fucker's helping
the homeless – we have reports of at least four nomadic

communes just within the city-limits. There's a growing
craze, it's proving resilient &

very very horribly
well organised.

They've been dubbed
the Shod Vagabonds

in The City, and
in the County

they call them

the Shoe People.
They call them

-selves The Tramping

Souls. We need
an aim, a goal,

a context-cue, & fast
managenital action.

These Tramping Souls are trampling society. No matter
how much it costs, because after

all it'll all

come from public coffers and not
of course from our own pockets, any

way as I
was saying

no matter
what & what

amount
of dosh

it costs
The Shod

Vagabonds
& their

blasphemous
false god

have got
to be

stopped!'

Metatron's Cube as Methuselah's Granny-Flat

mean

while

beyond

blurred suburb dreams

somewhere inner
city & dilapidated

Ol' Nanny Natter sits
in her thirty-year-old chair

she's been like this for weeks

sits as still
as glass spikes
cemented along a wall

for security

she does not blink
her skin is tight and gleams

she just sits

sits silently

rotting slowly

decomposing she will be

noticed only

by her stench next

month

Tom Cobbler's Troubling Vision

My Shoe Messiah
I am troubled
last night in the campfire

a fiery face
sang a song
to me

it was a female flame-face
and the gas-hiss sound
of Her voice was hot

& beautiful but also cold

I think I caught Her name
like of curl of flames
in my ears

a swirl of air like
So Far So Far So Far

I remember Her song
as if it were my own
but O My Messiah
how I doubt
it could be from me
I should be glad
for that doubt
for what follows
is surely blasphemy
but I'm so troubled that

I doubt I

could be from me
I'll trouble you

no more My Lord of Shoes

I can only hope

She means no harm

listen Her flames
are in my ears
again can you hear?

here is Her song:

Shoe Shit

what is it
that a shoe
digests

that a shoe
should produce
such muck?

remember
the poor
stray dog
with one paw
spoiled

with shoe shit

the stink
and how
the poor
mutt
could not
bear
to lick
his pads
& claws

clean again

do not forget
The Stained

Lost Dog.

•

then real's dream slashed
Sid's sides with

ice-talons his
scalp wobbled like

oil on river or
sea-water his face

slipped floppy as
a Dalí clock whilst on

his mind's muddy bank

a narcissus dripped yellow
coins that sank sizz

-zzling in his skull

his white bones burned
his brain & nerves

his footsteps hissed as his
shoes chewed him

his deadened head echoed

echoed a crow crawking
in a sepulchre echoed

a bank-vault door slammed

on abyss for a very
last time as

time lasts

•

It was black & raining
and I was following
the hot smell of foxes
from bin to bin through

Longgone's
Bombed-Out Pocket

Suddenly a white flash
of an owl swooped past
close to me I felt
on my skin the air
& rain droplets
the bird disturbed

and there it was I'd found
The Old Dark Hole of The House

soon as I entered
there was a stench
and a damp vibration
embraced me

it was some kind of abandoned
museum for shoes

in one corner of the dining room
on a table amongst mouldy boots
there was a decomposing man

utterly motionless

then with no sign
of approaching
I the Messiah of Shoes
was filled with a sudden

Presence of Patience

The Presence entered
the hole of my head
and the hollow of my heart

I just listened
I listened & let

the Motionless One

utter

The Three Songs of Lazarus Hollowshoes

Gone Song One

each wall of the house
is a bricked voice

each window sights
love & loss

these are the chairs
& these are the tables

& this is the bed
& this is the wardrobe

that all ran in
to the house out

of the rain

space keeps the place
for people who were

shapes of space
spaces that met

human smells

the ceilings will speak
blank patches amongst

cracks & cobwebs
the doors of the house

are gaps in the bricks
that promised to keep

the people's shapes
safe from the sky

& the breaths
of the land

see the chimney
pushes out shouts

and grey excretions
into the sky

Gone Song Two

the shoe
is a foot's cave

the leather shell
within which

the lowest
human part

resides

the creature
of shoe digests

the meat & bone
of Holy Journey

the laces & eyelets
are snakes

& wedding rings
as the hopes

of the rand
& tread leave

traces in mud
& dust dead

shoe leather squeaks
a live voice

as the foot flexes
maggot-like

in its carapace

out in the fields
herds of shoes

are rounded up
by jackboots

each empty shoe
cradles the death

of someone's song

each empty shoe
is a stomach full

of ghost

shoes are animal's
faces stitched &

twisted round
human feet

Gone Song Three

each wall of the shoe was a promise
the leather shell round a voice

each window the slowest human part

the creature of shoe digests The Site of Love
the chairs are the meat & bone of Holy Loss

the tables ran into journeys & laces
the house forms with the eyelids of snakes

rain keeps the place of rings & hopes

people who were the tread & the rand leave
shapes of people's spaces traced in dust & mud

spaces met with the human leather of the shoe
smells & ceilings squeak a living voice

speak with blank as the foot flexes

patches amongst cracked maggots & cobwebs
are the doors out into the fields of herds

in the house-gaps shoes are rounded up
the bricks that promised to jackboots

keep the people's shapes as empty shoe-holds
safe from the sky like the death of some song

breaths from land fill a stomach full of ghost
the chimney pushes out shoes & stitched faces

excretions into the sky twisted round human feet

a pink trainer
on its side
belonged

to a girl an hour ago

a thistle
slowly grows
to turn

it over

•

The Last & The Supper

And Sidney's Shod-Followers
did gather around a round

cobblers' workbench

(Alas under the bench
Tom Cobbler did inspect
his Messiah's soles
for defects)

And Sidney Realer did pull
from a troubling bubbling pot

The Cooked Shod

And The Cooked Shod was passed
from one shod follower to the next
And each soon-to-be New Shoe Apostle bit

into The Bitter Leather

And The Oil-Polished
Son of Shod
at The Last said

Chew for Eternity
Chew this Of Me

The Leather of Shoe
The Glue of Shoe
The Hole-Less Sole of Shoe
The Old Shoe Stew

This The Shoe-Host
of The Ghostly

For I am The Last
For I am The Load

who equals Two Tons
& is home
to The Two Tons' Toes

The Two Bone
Loadstones
that press
flesh & leather
together

to The Ground

For I am The Last
And in Olde
I am The Sole
of The Foot

For I am The Last
upon whom

The Leather
of The Living

are stretched
and nailed in place

For I am The Last
from whom
comes All Forms

of Shoe

The Lament of Judas Shoecutt

why my Shoe Messiah
did you show me

your wasted leather
your ripped stitches
why did you give

to me the black laces?

I was your shod brother
on road or in woods
why I loved you so Shoe Son

I have done as you bid me
taken the Goatskin Boots
to the Cobbler's Hatred
and I have been paid

for The Snapping of Laces

o I wish I had disobeyed
I wish I had merely kissed
your soles & your face
why me my Shoe Messiah?

see my left foot is for you
I've flashed my knife
through my chest

and pulled from my selves
the thumping red
I obeyed you

Shoe Messiah my eyes
are closing please
be there in the dark
Workshop of The Gone

be there for me please

see my left foot is for you
the pump I made for my
limping into forever is

The Shoe of My Heart

•

And an ugly crowd of middleys
did gather round Sidney

middleys – poeple of privilege

middleys afraid
for their cosy homes

middleys desperately needing their roads
free of the threat of the homeless

& jubilant shod-gangs

and so they did kick at Him
and spat on Him

(although not one
of them had been

brought up that way

they were middleys
they were never mean)

and they did begin
as if possessed

to chant at
The Shoe Messiah:

Unshoe The Shista
Unshoe The Shista

take off his shoes
take off his shoes

take his shoes
off of him
take his shoes
off of him

Fix His Shoes
Fix His Shoes
Fix His Shoes To Oak

LOOK!

one sock
is blue
one sock
is blue
the other
is red

the other
is red
there is

The Proof! kill

The King of The Shoes

Fosse Arrests The Shod One

Friends! Motorists!
I will attend to your fears
I do not come to bury ground
I come to praise roads
& erase the itinerant threat
remember roads are good
for The Globe

You know me Middleys
I am of All Ways
that are High

I am Anthony Fosse
Proph. John's Opposite
Fosse of The Agency
and it is my Job

to keep the streets
whether long
& straight or short
& curved

clear

I am The Street Keeper

and I keep
The Streets
neat & clean
Tarmarked
& safe

we all know
The Streets
are No Place

for New Shoe Strays

I keep Our Streets clear
surfaced & safe for tyres

not for Messiahs

Sidney is Brought Before Magistrate Potent Polish

So, You are The New Shoe
what should I do with you?

… [silence as just after scrying]

Speak Man or forever lace
your tongue tight.

… [silence as just after lightening]

Are you The New Shoe
is it true?
Do you do good?
Or as AZDA have asked
me to proclaim –
are you profane

are you a pretentious shoe fetishist?

What do you have to say
for your self
& your

allegedly stolen soles?

NOTHING!

Nothing?
No good shodding
will come of nothing.

Speak!

all I have done
is shoe those un-homed

All you now need do
to remain accepted
as part of Society
is publicly apologise
and take back the shoes
and say you are glad
for our riches and

glad for AZDA.

... [silence as after hammered iron]

Sidney I do not want
to condemn you, you
are a silly man
that is all, but
you have offended them.

You are a terror to them.

And I cannot defend –
I cannot join your mad
stolen-sole-shod parade
to be condemned with you.

Speak for Christ's sakes man, speak –
confess your sins,
say you're sorry.

...   [silence as just after dying]

Nothing.
Nothing I can do.
Nothing,
Son of Shod or Not.

I wash my hands
of Your Shoes.

The Shoefixation

(Being an account
of The Cruel Fixing
& a version
of a crucial fiction)

first they did scourge
the soles of his bare feet
with a fine brush
of orange copper wire

until his skin turned
into a plush mushy

red suede

And this was known
as The Excruciating Exfoliation

And secondly they did
fill his shoes with ashes
made from the burning
of his precious Red Sock

And they did put these
two shoes upon
each of his hands

And this was known
as The Love-Gloving of Shod

thirdly they did force
him upon his raw feet
to march

And he did feel the ground
And the connection
to it was electric

And this was known
as The Walk Over The World

fourthly they did forcefully
bring him to Car-Very Park

his two ash-filled shoes
were taken from Him
these two Too-New shoes
were fixed to

The Last Oak Standing

The Shoes At Last Fixed

with three steel nails
& a mile-long length
of yellow ribbon

And this was known
as The Skin's Fixing to Tree

And then they did deal
with Sidney Realer's
mortal frame

two dark cars
with smoky glass
were parked
on his palms

And his feet
were clamped
to a parking-meter
and the meter read:

PBMF

Penalty for Being
Momentarily Free

And The Agent
of The Highway

did paint yellow lines

lines side by side
lines twice
lines times
two

The Agent
did paint these
straight stigmata

of Double Yellow

upon The Shoeley One
from palm to palm
and from

head to foot

And O The Agent did turn
to the gathered & said:
behold

The King of The Shoes

Then Anthony Fosse
knelt down
To The Son of Shod

and spoke close
and almost
gently hissed
his last words to Him:

Y o u   T o e - R a g   Y o u

S h i t   L i t t l e   S h o e

And then they did leave
Sidney Realer supine & painted
on the Tarmarked Lot
of Car-Very Park

And Sidney
did utter

unto & into
the unknown

boundless Shoe of The Universe:

Why have you painted me so?

Forgive them Olde Shoe
for they do not know
the double they do!

O but You do
Olde Shoe
You knew

& You know
& You do

•

Crow
black tattered

jackboots flapping

attacked
& pecked

out

The Messiah's
soft eyes

Crow took
Shod's Eyes

into The Creaking
Oak's Crown

and so Crow ate
His Holy

Take Away

•

And for three days
did Sidney Realer suffer
the horror of the mocking

the insidious snickering
whispering in his ears
from certain solicitors:

No Fin No Wee
No Fin No Wee

No Win No Fee
where there's blame
there's a claim
No Win No Fee

hey Shoe Messiah
who could you sue?
give us a sign
give us a clue
hey who do you
wish would pay
for your shame?

give us our deeds today

and we'll sue
for you
give us permission
for us to use

your Brand Name
so we can sell
Messiah's Shoes®
o they'll go through
All Hell's Outlets

o they'll go

through AZDA
& Fleshgoze
for *every little*
helps us get richer o
they'll sell so
quick

    -ly & trick
    -ly like hot c
    -akes
    & snakes esc

    ape
    -ing The

    Fla
    -mes of Cali
    fawnian F
    -ires

so who will it be
Shoe Shod
who will you choose?
who will you sue?

we'll sue all souls

if it's your pleasure
we'll sue The Devil
and then go

for Gold
go for

your
God

even Eternity
can be sold
come on
Shoe Shod
give us our
Dosh
give us
All you've got
Go on Son
give us The Bread
give us Hell

it'll sell

give us our deeds

for as long
as it takes

The Song
to be sung

a deal
is a deal

until done

And the wicked did
go on dripping & dripping
their bile into Sidney

through his ears

And then Sidney in his thirst
did beg for water but

he got more torture & more voices ...

we interrupt this program
to bring you a news flash

a giant lorry-load of shoes
was overturned earlier
today on the long grey
motorway between

here & now

all exits to the past
and to the future

on both the charity-
& the hope-bound
carriageways

are now blocked

emergency services
are urgently seeking
volunteers to sweep
up the unusually huge
Pile of Shoes

... which vinegar
Sarson's or Samson's?

which butter
Utterly
or Beautifully
Buttery?

hey Shoey
is this fizz
Petpiss
Leprosee
or Choke?

speak Sweet Feet
what can you taste?

or is there a cat's
cradle of laces
& cracked shoe leather
packed around your
fattening tongue?

•

And Mandy Realer
And Marion Madder-Layne
Did weep together

The burning of baby-shoes

•

And at The Very Last
The British State Police
came to take Sidney away

but he had no eyes
to identify him by

so they let him go

the broken & blind
unshod ghost
of a man & messiah
painfully painted
with double-yellow lines

they let him go

he seemed more terrified
than terrifying
he was lame & blind
The Police & The State

played it down

please move along
nothing to see here
we've got business to do
we've got to deal
with the real
& the real's
public fears
we want no war
with someone
so wanting
move along
we need to get on
not with War on Him
nor with War on You

but we do do
dearly need
to get on with

War on Them

they let him go

let him be blown
lonely like a rag
in the winds

of disbelief
And he was lost

like an old sock

dirty & wet
on The Verge

of The World

buffeted
by the updrafts
of the Juggernauts

•

Revelation According to Sidney

O it was just after The Wedding
o just so momentarily

I glimpsed a grain of rice
I was the one who came near

it was at the back
of The Church
in The Well

-To-Do Village

at first I thought
I heard the words
of a sermon no one
could have written

I was mistaken
I know now
the words

could never be heard

however I did
I'm certain
encounter

The Tramp Known By No One

The Dog-Collared Tramp
forever in a Mack
and in a frenzy

dreaming of living

I saw clearly
crawling on his brow
the little glistening Shoe
-Shaped Beatle

and he did
in deeds
reveal to me

his secret

for he carried a jar
with a face in it

and the jar had a label
and written on the label

was a woman's name

The Tramp Known by No Man
at The Back of The Church

was no other than
the one who for long
into the dark night

darned socks

I knew him then
and I knew

he cared

especially when
pointing at The Hedge
he said:

Ah, look at all
The Prickly Holly

•

•

•

•

Blind Cinderella

@ The Shoddy Pond
in The Copse Beyond

Here & Then & Now & There

The Stunted Oaks hunch
round the black liquid disc
in the hollow
of The Old Bomb Hole

the failing orange light
of The Last Distant City
is a thin band between

The Dark Sky

& the Earth's horizon
yet the satsuma-light oozes
between the short trunks
& curly branches

of The Stunted Oaks

there are no leaves
for these are The Oaks
of The Apocalypse
that've shed The Acorns
of The Slip-Shod

Sidney has no eye

with which to see
the pale Clementine light
nor an eye
by which he may
be identified

Blind Sidney Realer
with naked bleeding feet
& cheek bones
blade-like beneath
his taught orangey-grey skin
his sockets as dark

as The Pond

Sidney can hear another
is lolling at The Pond's Edge
Sidney can smell
the other's shape & intent

o it

's Little Timothy Fisher
the strange little boy from
The Forgotten Estate
Tiny Sprat-Catcher Tim

is

by The Shoddy Pond
keeping Sidney company

and forever offering Him
sandwiches & apples
from The Last Packed Lunch

His Mum made
just before
The Blast

Sidney can smell the blood
slowly trickling down
the small boy's distorted leg

but The Lame Lad
is glad as he dips
his little rod
into the dark

slick disc

Suddenly Sidney feels a snail
slowly slide along the knife
-edge of his cheekbone
the snail slowly slips
into his left

hollow socket

and suddenly Sidney has
a swirl of brittle stone
for an eye

Sidney hears
the tension
in the shoelace tied
to the end
of The Lame Lad's
bending rod

The Shoddy Pond
quivers & gurgles

Sidney opens his
sour mouth
he begins to push

air through his throat

push push as if
he's giving
birth to first

words

ACKNOWLEDGEMENTS:

A very few parts of *Shod* have been previously dispersed, however the following literary organs are now thanked for having cast fragments:

The Coffee House, The Rialto, Under The Radar.

I am grateful for lines by Alice Oswald, quoted by Lermin Whiz-Shod & Peter Eaughost.

I'm most grateful to the following, who are not actually 'a following', but have shown some faith in *Shod* by way of encouragement and vital critical comments about some or all of the text:

Rob & Deb Cooper, Kerry Featherstone, John Gallas, Chris Jones, Luke Kennard, Geraldine Monk, Deborah Tyler-Bennett, Mary Reeler, James & Elaine Wheeler.

Special thanks to Jane Commane & Matt Nunn for such close reading of and careful critical comment about *Shod.* Bless you! Shoeven holds a place for you both.

Amazed thanks to Nikki Clayton for managing to bear the process of *Shod*'s creation, and also for her vital contribution.

Thanks to Nick Mott for telling me about his seeing a picture in *The Guardian* of a homeless journalist wearing the same shoes as his. And so, it is Nick Mott who is responsible for *Shod*'s genesis.

Polished / begat | Son of Shod / begat | · Eternity / begat | Of Me / begat |
The Leather of Shoe / begat | The Glue of Shoe / begat | The Hole-Less Sole of
Shoe / begat | The Old Shoe Stew / begat | The Shoe-Host of The Ghostly /
begat | The Load / begat | Two Tons / begat | The Two Tons' Toes / begat | The
Two Bone Loadstones / begat | Olde / begat | The Sole of The Foot / begat |
The Leather of The Living / begat | All Forms of Shoe / begat | The Lament /
begat | Judas Shoecutt / begat | Shoe Son / begat | · Goatskin Boots / begat |
Cobbler's Hatred / begat | The Snapping of Laces / begat | Workshop of The Gone
/ begat | The Shoe of My Heart / begat | Middleys / begat | The Shoe Messiah
/ begat | The Shista / begat | His Shoes / begat | His Shoes To Oak
/ begat | · LOOK! · / begat | The Proof / begat | The
King of The Shoes /begat| Fosse /begat| The Shod One /begat| Friends
/begat| Motorists / begat | The Globe / begat | All Ways / begat | High
/ begat | Anthony Fosse / begat | Proph John's Opposite / begat | Fosse of The
Agency / begat | Job / begat | The Street Keeper / begat | The Streets / begat
|Tarmarked /begat| No Place /begat | New Shoe Straps / begat | Our Streets /
begat| Magistrate Potent Polish / begat| The New Shoe /begat| Man / begat |
NOTHING! / begat | Society / begat | Christ's / begat | Son of Shod or Not /
begat | Your Shoes / begat | Shoe fixation / begat | The Cruel Fixing / begat |
The Excruciating / begat | Exfoliation / begat | Red Sock / begat | The Love-
Gloving of Shod / begat | The Walk Over The World / begat | Car-Very Park
/begat | Too New /begat | The Last Oak Standing / begat | The Shoes At Last
Fixed / begat | The Skin's Fixing to Tree / begat | Penalty for Being
Momentarily Free · / begat | The Agent of The Highway / begat | The Agent
/ begat | Double Yellow / begat | The Shoeley One / begat | The Son of Shod
/ begat | You Toe-Rag / begat | You Shit Little Shoe / begat | Tarmarked Lot
/ begat | Shoe of The Universe / begat | Olde Shoe / begat | · Crow / begat
| Shod's Eyes / begat | The Creaking Oak's Crown / begat | His Holy Take
Away / begat | No Fin No Wee / begat | No Win No Fee / begat | Brand
Name / begat | Messiah's Shoes® /begat| All Hell's Outlets /begat| Fleshgoze
/begat| The Flames of Californian Fires / begat | Shoe Shod / begat | The Devil
/ begat | Gold / begat | Dosh / begat | · All / begat | Go on Son / begat | The
Bread / begat | Hell / begat | Pile of Shoes / begat | Sarson's / begat |
Samson's / begat | Utterly / begat |Beautifully Buttery / begat | Shoey / begat |
Petpiss / begat | Leprosee / begat | Choke / begat| Sweet Feet /begat | The
Very Last / begat | The British State Police / begat | The Police & The State /
begat | War on Him / begat | War on You /begat | · War on Them / begat |
The Verge of The World / begat | Juggernauts / begat| Revelation /begat | The
Wedding / begat | The Church / begat | The Well-To-Do Village / begat | The
Tramp Known By NoOne / begat| The Dog-Collared Tramp / begat | Mack / begat
| Shoe-Shaped Beatle / begat | The Tramp Known by No-Man / begat | The Back
of The Church / begat | The Hedge / begat | Ah / begat | The Prickly Holly /
begat | Blind Cinderella /begat| @ /begat| The Shoddy Pond/ begat | The Copse
Beyond / begat | Here & Then & Now & There / begat | The Stunted
Oaks /begat| The Old Bomb Hole / begat| The Last Distant City /begat| The Dark
Sky / begat |Earth's / begat | The Oaks of The Apocalypse / begat | The Acorns of
The Slip-Shod / begat| Clementine / begat| ·Blind Sidney Realer / begat| The Pond
/ begat | The Pond's Edge / begat | Little Timothy Fisher / begat | Tiny Sprat-
Catcher Tim / begat | The Last Packed Lunch / begat | His Mum / begat |
The Blast / begat | Suddenly Sidney / begat | The Lame Lad's / begat | words

Kneeling Untied Slipped Off Neat Movement | But Her Cupped Tugged Tickled Lovely • Herself Me |Shelf Daring Air White | Her Underwear Huge Trainers| Back Daft Asked |Gabrielle Laughed| Gas Breath Smacked Last |Laughed Every Ad Colourless White |Line Laughed i As Kid Said If Fits • New Rests| Oaks Remnants In Trees As Forest County | Was Dubbed Blood | Sid's Slip of Earth |Sol World Now New Begins Which Sings| Pulls Hood | Reveal Red Tongue Resonating| Edges Bow Open | Throws Arrows | Shows Realer Dream | Him Grim | Mesmerising Tale | Listen Tale Lass | Cindy Had Glass|Shat As Strode Slashed Feet|Cindy Relative Wherever| Went Left | Trail Slip| Red Found Had Heart | Glass |Glass That Crazed | She Kissed Pussy of Purple | Re Rain Blood At Said Moral | This Slippers |Glass Allah Him! |Sandals Have Soles| Sakes' Philosophies Shon Glass Warm Souls | Man Brian His |Not Glass Just Naught | -Y Empty | Hollow Alone Was Followed | Felt Only So ⊖ | Love Will Only One Time Ever | Adam • Barn Woman Bag | Fert Waste Bothered Amazed Leather | From Tugging Stink a Shock Offering Unowned | Then Gently Shoe Removed Replaced Sock | One | Her Cunt Town-Name Glad | Found Shod Vagabond Layne • Sid's Son Heard | He Claimed Be Messiah Shoes | NO! Son One | Son Normal | Ordinary Any Son Admittedly | Be Naughty & Times | Odd Teens | Goth Punk Mod Python | Just Not Son| Shod's My One |Knees Pleaded Turn-Ups | Jeans' Tears | Out Fields |Barn Broken | Me Me Me Me | Will Forget Forget | When Dead Said | Mum | Was Son Lost Unshod | Mother NOTHING Word| Mum-Memento | Hope Remembering | Into Palm First Shoe | One Two | Keep Other | Secret • Where Grove Filled Club-Air | Muse-Tongue His Pages | His Pages Not Last | Now Sparks Verses | Leathery Bard Thinks Across Church | Sweet Eloise |Fatal Trail | Love-Bent Tacks | Stars Uh-Huh |You Shoe Above Below| Fottsteps Woods' Lyrics|Shapely Singer| Her Incarnation Big | Together An And | Latest Song : Moon Sounds Moun| Girls Done Shearsman Gown | Whore Sounds Read (|) Seed (|) Occupies (|) Eats (|) Fathers (|) Been Mimicry Moon-Anvil | Grain Sounds Undress Pain | Souds Moon Bleeding | Girls Done • Shoes Shoes | Polish Gloss | Sunshine-Buffed Name| Shoes Me|Run Through Alike | Daughters Beneath Abundant Solomon | Leather I | Laces So | Shod is Shod Right | Tight Cometh Upon Feet | Window See Flesh spoil | Tender Is Turn Mountain | Fast Shoedon |Spun Oak-Nestle Speaking Comely | Been Achilles' Lilies | Otters' Daughters Gleam | Cobbler Seals Strong ⊖ | One Make Bliss • Listen | If Really If | Take Shit | Grace May Stand All Saints Trudging Worlds' Tracts Passing Selves Through Shite |Soul Be Warned i Messiah Cannot |This Felt & Too Un-Poet Writing Wrote Who & Read Tragic Nasty Alliterating Shit | Dank Alley-World-City | Nearly Bleeding Old Girl-Bones | She Bruised Once | Head Bare Cigarette | Feet Rags | Her Passed and Stank | Piss-Shit-Stained Knees | Each Patella Wept Down Cheeks | She Head On |Smile Alley Me |Shoeherd Hurt Knees Healed | Me Bad Sad Helpless |Each Own Kind Known | Me Lord Unworn | Footwear Indeed Just Legally | Now Vow | Make Selves To Men Know | Say Bleed Enoch Old Old Need | Clapped Of Book Shearsman | Needle Thread Me | Thread DNA Names : Noah Metatron Solomon Even Man Mention Course Lord & Seen Millions | Seen Alone | Know Hole Between Legs | Sore Fire Miles Tramping Like Blackened Slipper Lost On Hardcore Beyond Hardshoulder | me Jesus | Weep See Instantly Names Know Nameless : Whore Blamed Game Baby Lone Maybe| Reached Fingers Gesture Of What Again Like Bag Wind | Hawthorn Windsor Name : sir sir sir & this sir sir sirs sir sir miles miles Travelled | Slot This Gold Fire Is Sophie's Hole | I Though Broken Stood Me | Face Infinite Terrible Consuming With Like Striking Tree | Mother From Son Mother-Fucker Purpose Apperance | Song Everyman's Inside Daughter | Lost World's Knowledge Here | Queen Down Upon Upon Be Fucked | Queen Old Occult Me She Always | Been Queen Obsrene Unseen | Finished Singing Walk | Wore Shoes' Miles |I Side Feet |Tears Me Met Other Song all Other Out |In Barn Bag Birth Blood •